Ferguson the Forgetful Frog

A Story About Dementia

By Dr. Paul J. Gerber

Illustrated by Veronica Geran Gerber

ISBN: 978-1533498380
ISBN-1533498385

OUR DEDICATION

This book is dedicated to the amazing people who cared for Helen, "R", and Peter

MY DEDICATION TO

____

A NOTE TO ADULTS

Talking to young children about dementia is quite difficult. It is not easy when adults have to talk about dementia. This book is intended to demystify the concept, the behaviors, and the feelings of the children who experience people with dementia first hand.

It is designed to be a catalyst for conversation, understanding and processing feelings. If children are not given the wherewithal to think about something new in their lives in productive ways, they reach their own conclusions.

When left alone to figure out a complex condition like dementia the outcome can be erroneous feelings. This can result in guilt, rejection and helplessness. The story of Ferguson the Forgetful Frog provides an opportunity for children to understand dementia so they can interact with their loved ones with care and understanding.

This is Ferguson the Forgetful Frog.
He is old and is not able to take care of himself.
He acts differently than he used to.

People all over the world are named Ferguson.
Dementia too is found all around the world. It means being forgetful and many other things. This story will explain it to you.

Every day Ferguson the Forgetful Frog lives in a courtyard of an assisted living building with bushes, plants and flowers. Assisted living is where older people go to live when they need a lot of help.

How did Ferguson get there? – no one knows. Ferguson knows – but guess what, he forgot! Ferguson has dementia.

Perhaps your grandma or grandpa has dementia too. If you can understand Ferguson the Forgetful Frog, then you can understand them better.

Ferguson has trouble remembering things...

What is your name?
How old are you?
Have you seen my watch?

Ferguson often seems depressed...

I am sad today.
I miss my own bed.
I feel like I am getting too old.
I have trouble doing things.

Ferguson seems tired a lot…

I cannot sleep at night.
I nod off when I sit for a long time.
Moving around wears me out.

Ferguson often gets confused...

I am not sure if I ate breakfast today.
Are you my son or my grandson?
How did I get here?

Ferguson has challenges feeding himself...

The food falls off my fork.
My shaky hand makes me spill.
The soup dripped in my lap.

Ferguson has difficulty with time...

What day is it?
Is it summer or winter?
Is my next meal dinner or breakfast?

Ferguson dresses funny…

My polka dot pants do not match my plaid shirt.

I am wearing two different socks.

Ferguson cannot walk very well...

Other times I need a walker.
I am too weak to walk anywhere.
Sometimes I need to be in a wheelchair.

Ferguson has trouble going to the bathroom...

I need help when I have to pee.

I think I had an accident.

My diaper is wet again.

OOPS!

Ferguson sometimes has bruises...

*My skin is so sensitive.
I bump my legs a lot
on the furniture.
When people help me
they hold me too tight.*

Sometimes Ferguson gets sick...

I do not feel well today.
My heart is giving me trouble.
It is hard for me to move my arms and legs.

Ferguson does not remember special days of the year...

When is your birthday again?

Did I miss Thanksgiving this year?

How old am I this year?

Ferguson gets embarrassed often...

Sorry, I cannot walk very fast.

I cough a lot when I drink.

I confuse you and your brothers and sisters.

Now that you know more about Ferguson the Forgetful Frog here are some things to remember. Most important Ferguson the Forgetful Frog is different than most people who get old.

1. He loves people. Sometimes it is hard for him to show it.

2. Ferguson cares about you, just in very different ways.

3. Ferguson's condition might become worse in time. But his love for you will still be inside him.

4. Ferguson's memories now live in YOU to hold on to for him. That is very special!

Ferguson has lived a long time. His life has gotten more difficult. Ferguson would be sad if people would not remember him smiling and doing what happy frogs do every day.

He lives in an assisted living courtyard surrounded by bushes plants and flowers.

He is happy for every day he sees the sun rise.

Dr. Paul J. Gerber is Professor of Special Education and Disability Policy at Virginia Commonwealth University. He holds the Ruth Harris Professorship of Dyslexia Studies in the School of Education. He earned his Ph.D. in special education and school psychology at the University of Michigan.

Veronica Geran Gerber split her career and interests working as a graphic designer in television and then teaching high school art. She has art degrees from the University of Michigan and Virginia Commonwealth University.

Made in the USA
Middletown, DE
06 July 2022

68614974R00029